Wit & Wisdom for Widows

Beginning Anew

By

Barbara Whitman Gaeta & Susan Whitman

ISBN: 1-40330-167-0

This book is printed on acid free paper.

1st Books - rev. 03/12/02

Acknowledgments

We want to acknowledge Susan Pilgrim for her help and support for bringing our dream to reality.

We acknowledge our husbands, Manny Gaeta and Dick Seidenzahl, for their support and encouragement.

We're grateful to Paul Burt of 1st Books Library who helped us see this project to fruition.

We honor those widows who attended our first workshop and shared their experiences.

Dedication

For all widows

And in honor and memory of Richard W. Whitman, husband and
father,
who brought joy to our lives.

Table of Contents

Preface

Richard Whitman died suddenly while taking a shower in 1986. Instantly Barbara Whitman became a widow. We'd been married for 40 years. How was I to live without him? I was devastated. I was lost.

Unfortunately, I'm not alone. Whether our status changes without warning or is expected because of illness, widows are not prepared to deal with what comes after marriage and after the death of a mate. Through no volition of our own, we join more than 11 million widows in the United States. We are thrust into a life and often a lifestyle not of our choosing.

One of the phenomenon we've come across is there's no concerted effort by society or even religious institutions to meet the needs of widows. Why is that? Being a widow is still taboo. We don't talk about it. We hope it doesn't happen to us. We're not encouraged to prepare for the likelihood, even when it's imminent. Even with all of society's emphasis on inclusiveness and diversity, we discriminate against and take advantage of widows. We don't encourage the widow to find a new life. The reality is that a woman married to someone her age or older will likely outlive him, thus joining the widow community.

Whereas this is undeniably a tragic time in life, it's also a significant opportunity to create life in a new way, to explore opportunities that weren't available to you before, to reinvent yourself if you wish…to begin anew. Had Richard not died, there are so many experiences I would have never had. [You'll have to read the rest of this book to learn about them!] Had he not died, Susan would approach her marriage to a man 14 years her senior without awareness.

We suffered the pain of loss as a wife and a daughter. We refused to get stuck in the pain. We grew closer together as we explored this strange new world. We developed a new understanding of life. We felt a renewed appreciation for our husbands. Susan accepted her likelihood of becoming a widow.

We recognize there's a specialness about widows. They have a wisdom that surpasses that of the wise and well meaning healer. We believe widows are to be revered, sought after for their perspective. We also believe widows have an obligation to help other widows along the way in their journey to a new life.

We wrote this book, *Wit & Wisdom for Widows: Beginning Anew*, to offer an uplifting and entertaining approach to living through widowhood. We tell our stories with humor, the essential survival tool for some of fate's cruel blows. We laughed at ourselves because getting to know ourselves better and each other more deeply was no piece of cake. Sometimes we didn't like what we found out. Isn't that right, Mom? We admit that what happened wasn't funny at the time it occurred; but in retrospect, our memories have become lighter, serving as friendly reminders of life's paradoxical wit.

In this book, we don't tell you how to be a good, socially acceptable widow. We encourage you to break the mold. We challenge you to face and move beyond your grief and fears and deal with your issues head on. We empower you to take action, to do what's best for you. And, hopefully, we inspire you to walk a new walk and live a new life by beginning anew everyday.

We wrote this book for married woman also so they can explore widowhood without fear or shame and prepare for the likely future. We wrote this book for friends, family members, and healers so they can increase their understanding of the widow's journey and offer it as a resource to widows close to them.

I was taught that when one door closes another opens. My experience has shown me that this is true. The door slammed shut on the life I knew. The path awaiting me was unknown. There was and is still today no going back. The path I chose led to another rewarding and fulfilling life, one that was different from the rich and satisfying life I shared with Richard. Humor has carried me along the bumpy path. Humor has sustained me through this scary journey. When I fell by the wayside, and I did many times, I got up and trod on. I stuck to my commitment to a new life and found the rainbow I was seeking.

Good luck on your journey. We're certain you'll find your own rainbow along the path.

Barbara Whitman Gaeta & Susan Whitman
Los Gatos, CA & Pacific Grove, CA
March 2001

Introduction

I was driving up a long and winding one-lane road into the Santa Cruz mountains. If I could have turned around, I would have. "You're really crazy," I kept thinking. "Well, it looked really nice on the television program," I'd respond. I was driving on automatic pilot, scared to death. I'd never done anything like this before...and was certain I'd never do anything like this ever again. I had no idea that this drive would change my live forever.

At the gatehouse, I asked if this was the place. A nice young woman assured me it was and told me she was glad I was here. Then she said, "Barbara, just put your clothes in the trunk of your car and bring that towel we told you about with you." I hesitated for a moment, then said to myself, "Well, I'm here. So, why not?" and took off my clothes, put them in the trunk, grabbed the beach towel, put on my big hat and sunglasses.

When I returned to the gatehouse, the young woman was waiting to give me the tour. After getting help down the stairs from a male guest, I realized this is a really nice place. I felt like I was in the Garden of Eden. It was quiet and peaceful. It was really beautiful. It didn't seem to matter that no one was wearing clothes. Clothing is optional here. I felt very safe.

I became a regular. Spending time at the naturist club gave me a great feeling of freedom. *This is the way I am. I accept me. I accept you the way you are.* I was free to be alone and quiet or to engage in conversation with those who welcomed interaction.

One Thursday, which became my regular day, I was swimming in the upper pool and heard Bill, a friend I'd made on previous visits, call out, "Barbara, come join us." He and a tall Latin man were sitting in the hot tub. Bill introduced me, "Manny, this is the friendliest lady you'll ever meet. Say 'hello' to Barbara." Obviously a bit shy, Manny extended his hand, greeted me with his million dollar smile, and said 'Hello, I'm Manny.' I was hooked. My first thoughts were, "What a handsome man! He looks just like Caesar Romero."

Manny and I spent the rest of the day talking, getting to know one another. I learned that he had been a long time member of the club. He was very comfortable in our surroundings. We found that we had much in common and really enjoyed each other's company. At the end of the day, we exchanged telephone numbers. I felt giddy, like an adolescent schoolgirl. I didn't think he would really call, and I was hoping beyond hope that he would. And, he did. He asked me to meet him at the club the next Thursday.

About three weeks after we first met, Manny was standing in the corner of the quiet pool when I arrived. As I was swimming around, I watched this quiet, gentle man. I was gathering my courage to approach him, to ask him the question that was on my mind. So finally I swam up to him and asked, "Do you like to hug and kiss?" With obvious surprise, he responded, "Well, yes, I do." "Me, too," I said and gave him a big hug. After a few minutes, I swam up to him again and shamelessly asked, "Do you like to make love?" He directly said, "Yes, I do." I gave him a big hug and a gentle loving kiss. I looked into his warm eyes and said, "I'm glad to know you, Manny." Something grand was unfolding!

Because he lived in San Jose and I lived in Oakland, our time together was limited and very special. We met every Thursday, talking, listening, touching, hugging, and kissing. I discovered that Manny was a man I could love. Each time we were together over this three-year period, I realized God had sent me a gift. God had sent another soul mate to share my new life with.

We began getting together outside of the naturist club, having dinner on Sunday nights to cap off the weekend. Finally, I couldn't stand it any longer. So, I asked him, "Are you going to marry me?" "Yes," he replied. "When?" "This year" was his response. "December 31st?" "No, before that." "Day after Christmas?" "OK."

So on December 26th, I married the second love of my life…starting a whole new life with a man I love, to whom I'm eternally committed, who happens to be 12 years my junior.

I tell you this story about meeting Manny to show you that if a woman in her sixties can create a new life for herself, so can you. I didn't join the naturist club to find a mate. Doing so was one of the unexpected outcomes of my doing something different. Neither do you have to go to a naturist club to find a mate, nor do you have to find a new mate at all to live a new life. You do have to be willing to put aside old ways of thinking and old ways of doing things. You do have to be willing to embrace adventure and experience the unfamiliar. You do have to be willing to make choices that are different from ones you've made in the past. You're in a different place in your life, and it's time to experience life differently…to begin anew.

Chapter 1
Walk Their Way? No Way!

Wear black. Hide your feelings. Attend your husband's funeral incognito. Cover your face with a veil. Throw yourself onto the burning pyre of your dead husband. Be stoic. Stay inside the house for a year. Commit suicide. Be helpless. Deny your feelings. Succumb to the sexual advances of your husband's brother. Put living on hold. Don't ever cry. Move in with your children. Cry all the time. Move in with your in-laws. Wallow in your grief. Drape your home with black fabric. Pay penance. Allow others, including family members, to take advantage of you. Blame yourself. Deny your sexual urges. Disappear. Grieve until you die.

Whew! We don't know what you're thinking, but all of these options sound totally dismal to us. These are a culmination of expected behaviors of the conventional widow throughout various cultures of the world. Why would you want to be anything like her? We say, "NO WAY!"

We invite you and encourage you to break the mold of what widows are suppose to act like. Just because such behaviors are traditional and expected doesn't mean you should engage in them. Sure, you're going to grieve. You're going to be sad. You're going to make changes in your life. But, whatever you do, you should do it because you want to, not because others expect, want, or force you to.

Imprinted in most of our brains is the image of Jacqueline Bouvier Kennedy at the funeral of her husband, John F. Kennedy. She wore black. She wore a veil. She didn't cry in public. She was a silent stoic onlooker of the events that followed her husband's death. So when we think about what's a widow to do, how's a widow suppose to act, her image instantly fills our minds.

You have the freedom to choose. You can wear black or red or purple for all we care. We want you to do what feels right for you. If you want to laugh and cry and tell jokes, go for it. This is your life, albeit changed forever, and you can live it anyway you want.

Picture this:

A widow at her husband's wake is laughing with others in a courtyard. She's wearing a light blue dress that reveals all of her femininity. Intermittently she sheds a tear. Rock and roll music, the deceased's favorite, is playing in the background. The fragrance of flowers fills the room. Delicious food is abundantly available. This is an uplifting celebration of life...the dead husband's and the new widow's. She's celebrating the life she knew and the one that's about to unfold before her. She's showing appreciation for her beloved and is excitedly anticipating what she can now create. She's both sad and joyful. She's grieving and moving forward in life in her own way.

Hmmm....what if this were the model of how to be a widow. It's only one idea...it's not anymore the ideal than is throwing yourself on the funeral pyre. What is ideal is that she's celebrating life and expressing appreciation for what has been and what is to come. There are countless ways to live your life as a widow. You have to determine what being a widow means to you. Remember widowhood is about living, not about waiting to die.

In creating your own life, one that makes sense to you, we strongly encourage you to make sure there's joy where there's sorrow, there's love where there's anger, and there's healing where there's pain. Don't be concerned about others' expectations, their judgments, or their thoughts. Don't concern yourself if you're grieving and moving in the socially acceptable way. Remember you know what's best for you, even if it takes some time to figure that out.

This is still your life, more so than ever before. Good fortune awaits you as you begin anew.

Chapter 2
Condolences & Congratulations

It may seem odd to think of condolences and congratulations in the same thought. 'Condolences' makes sense, right? You've experienced one of the most debilitating tragedies in life. You have lost life as you know it.

We do offer our sincere condolences. We've been there. We know how it feels to lose the love of your life, to lose the man you've been joined with so intimately, to lose a life that's familiar and comfortable. We know you feel all alone in this world, but you're not alone. You're joining the ranks of more than 11 million women in the U.S. We know that this fact doesn't really give you the comfort you crave. We know you want to be consoled. We know you want to wake up from this nightmare. We know you're asking the question, "Why me?" We know there's no answer to that question.

But what about 'congratulations?' There's nothing logical or empathetic about congratulating a woman who has just lost her mate, who has just lost her life, who has just had her world turned upside down and inside out. Or is there?

We congratulate new brides and grooms. We congratulate new graduates. We congratulate those with new jobs. We congratulate new retirees. We congratulate those who have achieved a success. We congratulate those who have realized a dream. Notice that we congratulate those who are embarking on a new phase of life. We congratulate those who are beginning anew.

So, doesn't it make sense to offer the widow congratulations? For indeed, if anyone is beginning anew, it must be the widow. In her new topsy-turvy world, achieving a sense of mental, emotional, and spiritual stability will be a much valued accomplishment. AND, beginning a new life, even though it isn't of her volition, is something to be acknowledged, a feat to be congratulated.

In your grief, we know that you'll slip in and out of pity for yourself, often getting stuck in pity's quagmire. We also know that as long as you sink deeper and deeper into that quagmire, you'll miss the newness of life, the experience of regeneration, and the ability to find new meaning in life. As long as you're hosting that pity party, you won't be able to accept any other invitations, to take the first step to begin anew.

It sounds like too much effort, doesn't it? A breathing corpse. Being manipulated by others. Full of dread. Attached to a life that exists only in your memory. Now that sounds appealing! But, hey, you have free will. So if you really want life to be this way, close this book and put your life on the proverbial shelf.

However, life goes on…with or without you. So, snap out of it! Seize this new opportunity to create a new life, one that would not have been possible if your mate had not made his transition from this world.

When you come to think about it, there are some benefits to being a widow. Like what? Well, my first positive thought after Rick died was *I don't have to ask anyone about anything I want to do.* You don't have to tell anyone where you're going. You don't have to cook meals or clean up the house. You don't have to feel compelled to be by your mate's side every moment. You can do what might be considered crazy things without judgment. You can sleep until noon. You can stay up all night. You don't have to compromise. You don't have to listen to his familiar incessant snoring...could Rick snore? No North Wind was a match for how he could move the drapes in our bedroom! You don't have to share the holidays with people you really don't like to be around. You can do anything you want to. Now, there's some real value in the freedom you're granted when you become a widow. So, rather than bemoaning your fate, look at the situation in a different way. Celebrate the best things about being a widow...and capitalize on them.

We're adamant about uncovering the value and excitement in living. We're jubilant about the new experiences that await you. We understand your hesitation to take the risk to move forward. We know, without any doubt, that unless you take the risk, you'll miss the best parts of living.

Won't you come with us on this journey? Won't you let yourself glimpse into a greater understanding of what your new life can be?

Come along as we share the wit and wisdom in life that we uncovered during our journey, our new walk in life.

Chapter 3
How Our Walk Began

Although my mother had been married for almost 40 years, she was only 56 when she became a widow. I was a newly wed at 36. Over the years, our mother-daughter relationship matured, yielding an adult friendship. We always had fun together. We shared a deep mutual admiration and respect for each other.

Around the time my father died, Mom liked to brag [she still does!] about her successful daughter who was a partner in a floral business and was an elected city councilperson. I, too, am continuously proud of my mother's the-kids-are-gone-now career success. There's no doubt about it. Mom is truly a self-made woman. Over the years, she struggled through many financial challenges to maintain a secure family life in spite of my father's epilepsy. She was the consummate volunteer. She was always, and still is, so friendly and funny. She glowed with pride in her Prince Charming, my dad.

It's a bit peculiar. Whenever the thought of my parents' mortality crossed my mind, I always imagined Dad alone. For some reason, I figured Mom would go first, maybe due to an accident or just burning herself out. I feared her leaving the most because I always felt my dad was so dependent on her. I was sure that he would die of a broken heart if anything happened. Well, maybe that's an exaggeration; however, I knew he would find life difficult without her. I knew Mom would be sad if Dad went first, but I'd been noticing that her newfound freedom as a career woman had afforded her a new

7

independence…and she thrived! Yes, Mom would be sad, but I was fairly certain that she wouldn't be immobilized without Dad.

One of Mom's most remarkable gifts is that she's an expert on relationships. I credit her for the sound advice she offered me about personnel matters in my business and about political conundrums. She always had wise words to share and helped me get a good perspective on a difficult situation. She made me think clearly about behaviors and look at possible outcomes. This gift she has was the reason for her success as a manager and trainer of volunteers. She's a great communicator, and everyone who meets her feels instantly comfortable. She has an entertaining knack for treating strangers like new friends.

Role Reversal—The Daughter Becomes the Mother

In a blink of an eye, our roles reversed on the day of Dad's death…neither of us even noticed. There was no conscious exchange of roles or responsibilities. Mom's loss seemed so much greater than mine. I put all of my energies into being "the good daughter." This is exactly what I'd observed her doing for her own mother, who only months before lost her husband, Mom's Dad, my grandpa. So, to carry out my newly self-assigned mothering role, I wanted to anticipate her every mood and need. I wanted to be there for her and I was, even to my own detriment.

For the first few days after Dad's death, I stuck to Mom like glue. Even though it was very hard for me to stay away from my flower shop business, I felt compelled to be with Mom. And, I felt I was doing it by myself. Unfortunately, retail stops for no one! So, my partner and friend, Paula carried on. Although she was experiencing her own grief, her loving support kept the cash register ringing. Because my husband had his own business to run, he couldn't go with me to Oakland. I had a full calendar, so many commitments—business, meetings, and projects. Yet, my world stopped in suspended disbelief while Mom and I tried to figure out what to do now that Dad was gone.

In retrospect, I'd say the contrast of our lives was extreme. I so wanted to comfort Mom. I wanted to protect her. I wanted to make decisions for her, thinking that I knew what was best for her. Little did I know just how naïve I was! I gave what I considered to be gentle advice to support her emotional needs. I'm certain my grandmother's reaction to Dad's death influenced my behavior. She had fallen into her own pit of grief and had nothing left over for her own daughter, my mother. Her behavior was completely unexpected. We later learned that it wasn't nearly as unusual as it seemed. We found that relatives, when reacting to widows, can be judgmental, condescending, and downright rude. The irony is that I was trying to play a role that I had no experience with…I had never been a mother. I had always been a little girl around my mom, even as an adult…until now. My dad was gone, and the little girl in me went with him.

In my efforts to mother and comfort, I created a relationship of dependence. I helped Mom find an apartment in the town where I lived. I subsidized her rent. I introduced her to my friends and business contacts. No surprise...they all loved her instantly! To further create a dependent relationship, I gave Mom a part-time job at the flower shop. I don't know which of these actions constituted the biggest mistake. Together they created a HUGE MISTAKE, which prolonged the grieving process and severely strained our relationship.

At the time, these actions seemed like fine ideas. I was tiring from the two and a half-hour drive to see her at least every other weekend. She'd always been my best salesperson at the shop on Mother's Day. It had been hers and Dad's tradition of coming down to help me out almost every holiday. The customers loved her happy and friendly personality. They found comfort in her suggestions for gifts. Who wouldn't want advice on what to buy mom on Mother's Day from a real live mom in the flower shop?

She's Making Me Crazy!

Well, this sure-fired great arrangement deteriorated quickly from the start. Whereas I initially wanted to be helpful and comforting, I couldn't maintain the same level of attention that I'd given Mom right after Dad died. I had created an expectation that I was no longer willing nor able to met. Mom was hurt. She wanted me to call her frequently. She was angry. She wanted to be included in my social life. Mom was making me crazy! I wanted her to get a life, preferably one I didn't have to orchestrate. And, I felt tremendous guilt. I was supposed to nurture and support her. I was her mother, I mean daughter, after all!

I sought counsel from an Episcopal priest. He met with Mom and me to discuss how she could get her needs met in other ways. I told her the truth. I told her what she was doing was driving me nuts! She didn't want to hear it. She became angrier. I suspect her feelings of abandonment fueled that anger. She'd been abandoned by her father, her mother, her husband, and now, her daughter…in such a short amount of time.

Disheartened, I visited the priest again. He helped me bring the situation into perspective. His words comforted and encouraged me. He advised, "Susan, your mother is still a vital woman with great skills and a lot of experience. She'll be able to take care of herself. She's just afraid. You may have to let her go in order to get her back. When you let go, you're expressing your faith in her ability to get her life together on her own. And, eventually, she'll feel very good about doing that."

Cutting the Cord

I knew I had to cut the cord if I wanted to maintain my own sanity. On the day I went to see her, I felt an unsurpassed inner peace. The day seemed somewhat surreal, like watching myself in a movie. Calmly and without tears, which was a first for me—Mom and I cried at everything, I told her I'd no longer help her with the rent and that she no longer worked at the shop. I told her that I loved her and knew that she'd be able to make it on her own. I told her I had to release the parachute and that I'd always be rooting for her. *How could I be so cruel? How could I treat my own mother this way?*

The depth of her hurt and anger with me was immeasurable…So deep that she didn't speak to me for almost a year. During this period, she expressed her feelings by writing some very angry letters, demanding that I return everything she had ever given me.

Fortunately, the priest was absolutely right. Her transformation was amazing. She picked herself up and started a new life. And, well, the rest is history…

Chapter 4

Beginning Your New Walk, Your New Journey

Taking a walk, a journey is a familiar experience, isn't it? You've been on lots of journeys—to visit family, to explore new places, to engage in business matters. Some journeys have been joyful. Others have been obligatory. However, this journey from widow to self-assured woman is unlike any journey you've experienced. You're starting this journey from the depths of hell and, if you'll allow the journey to do so, it will take you to the heights of heaven.

This journey will be the most important one you'll ever take. For if you don't take this journey, you'll cease to exist—figuratively and, eventually literally. If you want to know your true self and move forward in life, you must embark on this journey.

This journey is a new one. Now, keep in mind that *new* doesn't mean that it's better than the old. New does mean that it'll be different. You'll notice that fear will be your frequent traveling companion, particularly when the allure of enjoying the present and anxiously anticipating a joyful future emerges. The past will invoke fear along the path because it doesn't want to be forgotten. Not to worry…extricating or tampering with your memories is not a part of this journey. However, releasing your attachment to them so that you can move forward is essential.

What Does Death Mean Anyway?

Part of this journey involves exploring what you believe about death. We naturally reexamine long held belief systems during the anger stage of grief. As for me, I wanted to know where my daddy had gone. In my exploration, I came full circle. I moved from being a Sunday School Christian to the resolute skeptic to indulging in the Eastern, mystical, and reincarnation, finding my way to embrace Christian rituals anew. There was suddenly new meaning and a new experience with the power of the Spirit. I shed tears of joy and thanksgiving for the unconditional love and comfort God provided for me in the human form of church members. The words of the old hymns held real meaning for me. Their music gave new wings to my spirit.

The Devil Becomes an Angel

When we lose our mate, in retrospect, he somehow becomes more than he ever was in real life. I'm reminded of the saying, "Died a devil, but became more and more of an angel as time went on." My sweet husband, Rick, was not perfect. As time passed, his imperfections fell by the wayside. I was in love with the way I dreamed he was. To know that I had had a perfect husband was a great comfort to me. So, in beginning a new journey, I had to put away fantasy and seek out the facts. The fact was that Rick was gone…forever. I was comforted knowing that our wonderful memories would be with me…forever.

It's Time to Get Ready

So to begin anew, remember that new is just that, not better, not worse, but new, different. Wisdom reminds us that 'because you have loved and loved well, you have the capacity to love again and again.' In some way, the new is a testament to your past life. I like that. Acknowledging this truth empowered me to feel like a self-assured woman instead of a woman without a husband.

A smart woman never starts a new journey without the necessary things to help her complete it. Would you go into the desert without water? Girl, it's time to get ready. Here's what you need:

→ *Adjust your mindset.* This adjustment will allow new opportunities to present themselves. Remember that you are in charge of your life—not your friends, your children, your parents, no one but you. You don't have to ask anyone about anything you want to do.

→ *Laugh!* Ha! Ha! Ha! No departed loved one would like to see our lives devoid of laughter. There will be times of tears, and there will be times of laughter. Laughter is good medicine, helping you and others heal. Practice laughing... Rent funny movies. Watch children play at the park. Try on silly hats in the department store. Laugh out loud at the funny parts in a book. Watch the silly things your pet does. Laugh at the silly things you do...We did and still do. Let yourself roar!

→ *Take advantage of decision making opportunities.* The decisions you make will impact the remainder of your journey. Remember that only you know what's best for you. Others will tell you they know best...they don't. Even in writing this book, we don't know what's best for you. We provide you with information and encouragement, and, hopefully, our words will awaken your inner spirit to do what's for your greatest benefit.

→ ***Trust yourself to make the right decisions for you.*** Time will tell you when you're ready to move on. It may take a few months. It can take a year. But, if you're still in the 'widow' mode into the second and third year, you need a shove down the path! We're here to help.

→ ***Fuel your desire to move forward even when it's easier to stay in the past.***

→ ***Solicit and secure support.*** Identify the friends and family members who will help you meet your needs. Allow them to comfort you. Get to know others who can help you along your way. Seek out spiritual guidance.

→ ***Fine tune your trust in the Universe and your belief in God.*** Acknowledge the inner strength that you've been blessed with to move forward in spite of difficult circumstances.

→ ***Allow yourself to create your life's map as you walk down the new path.*** Be open to all sights and sounds you encounter along the way.

Your experiences, emotional strength, spiritual guidance, and relationships prepare you to begin the journey and sustain you along the way. The journey begins with the first step, with knowing that life goes on and requires your active participation. As you journey from the past into the present, you find that you must leave behind those relationships, attitudes, perceptions, and beliefs that hold you back, that no longer serve you, that you've outgrown, that you no longer see as true for you.

While on this new road, you'll look back, a natural thing to do. Glance. Remember. Then turn around and move on. Leaving behind the past doesn't mean it never existed or that you must never think of it. Leaving behind the past means you take the richness, the experiences, and the lessons you've learned to enhance your present life and to take you into a new future.

When the path you're on leads to a dead end, reflect on how you got to where you are, why it's a dead end, then take action to right your journey. Sometimes you'll find that people will walk with you. At other times, you'll be alone because the path narrows and there's only room for one.

In the reflective mirror of the past, we see ourselves in a different light. When we shine the light of the present on what has been, we're creating opportunities for a new beginning. Once we take the meaningful from the past, we can easily move with greater ease into the next experience of the present. We can easily move with greater ease into the future where life renews itself continually.

Maybe your journey includes a new job, new friends, a change in location, or a new perspective from treasured friends. You're in charge. There are things I never dreamed of that are happening in my life now. Rick would be the first one to rejoice with me.

Here I am in a new life with a wonderful man and another chance to love and be loved again. Your journey may or may not include a new man. Make every moment you have on this Earth count…BIG time.

You've already read about how our walk began in Chapter 3. In the pages that follow, it's likely you'll recognize where we've been. It's likely you'll connect with our experiences. Read on to learn how wit carried us through the rough places in the road and lifted our spirits to the heavens.

Chapter 5

Walking Away From the Past

My friend made a bold decision. She wanted to keep the treasured memories of her husband and the father of her children. Yet, preserving their traditional holiday activities with his obvious absence didn't seem quite right. She realized the family would be focused on the loss, not on the possibilities of the present and future. She knew it was time to walk away from the past. She decided to take the whole family on a cruise at Christmastime.

The sudden death of her husband, killed in front of their house while jogging, was devastating. She felt like she had no legs. In spite of that terrifying sensation, she forced herself to take steps. She knew if she stopped moving the excruciating pain would keep growing. She forced herself to walk away from the past, to walk in a new way. Each step gave her renewed vigor for a new life.

Angel in Disguise

Both Susan and I were so stunned about Rick's death. We kept thinking, kept hoping that this was just a bad dream and that we'd hear Rick's voice and see his face again. We were immobilized. When I called my best friend, Ann, to tell her the news, she flew from San Diego to Oakland at once. She made all the arrangements for Rick's service and cremation. She gave us such comfort and support at a time when we needed them the most.

Ann and I share a very special bond. We met many years ago when we were working for the Red Cross on the docks, serving coffee and donuts to servicemen who were going overseas. While we were talking into the wee hours of the morning, we realized we lived close to one another. When she told me her last name, I remarked that our paperboy had the same last name. Her immediate response was, "Isn't he awful?" And, he truly was. Rick would call to inquire where his paper was and Andy would reply, "Did you look on the roof or under the bushes next door?" Andy drove Rick crazy! Ann and I became like sisters, supporting each other over the years. So I really wasn't surprised that she came to take care of the logistics surrounding Rick's death and to take care of me. That's what true friends do for one another. She's most certainly my best friend, an angel in disguise.

→ *Consider…*

1. Allow others to help in ways they choose. This is no time to be self-sufficient.

2. Receive the comfort that's offered. Sink into it. Know that you'll reciprocate your friend's kindness somewhere in the future.

3. Express your gratitude. Show your appreciation in whatever way it makes sense for your relationship. Sometimes a simple 'Thank You' is sufficient. Sometimes it's a card or gift. You'll know what's right for your relationship.

If Only…

If only I hadn't gone to Susan's that Sunday, I could have intervened and Rick might still be with me today. There are lots of times after the initial shock of loss that I played this 'If Only…' game. Why didn't I stay home that day? I would have been there. If you're playing this game like I did, you may be noticing that you're making yourself sick…that you're wallowing in pity, that you're attached to the past. We don't have as much control over things as we'd like to have. I believe things happen for a reason even if it's never revealed. Perhaps one day it'll make sense; however, I decided that life must go on.

→ *Consider…*

1. If you let it, guilt can eat you up…fast. "If Only…" is a futile game. Rid yourself of any guilt you feel by writing a letter of all the "If Only…" sentiments. Place the letter in an envelope. Set it on fire [responsibly!] and watch it burn. Watching the burning will put the guilt to rest. USE EXTREME CAUTION! Don't burn yourself, your belongings, or the house down!

2. Avoid regrets in the future by doing those things that make sense for you now. Don't put off doing what makes you happy. Listen to your intuition.

Loss Comes in Too Many Packages

Mom has experienced many types of loss. She lost her husband through sudden death. She sat by her father's bedside while he suffered a short illness. She had time to say goodbye and witness his peaceful passing. Mom also endured the long and painful deterioration of her own mother for more than 10 years. It was the long goodbye that wore her down, making her wish for death to come and end the day-to-day pain she experienced. No matter how the loss occurs, the widow is faced with the demands of a thoughtless world that keeps moving, ignoring her tragic and painful loss.

➔ *Consider…*

1. Look for the JOY that's hidden in every painful moment.
2. No one gets out of this world alive. Death comes to each of us. You, too, will die some day. Remind yourself of this truth. Since death is an eventual reality, celebrate each day shamelessly.
3. Create a ceremony of farewell for your husband. Mark the end of the relationship with a photo album that represents the many stages of your relationship.

I'm Not Hungry…for Food, Anyway

Eating is an immediate problem for widows. For a long time, I didn't want to eat anything, even though friends and family said, "Eat something. You'll feel better." I really didn't want to feel better. Besides, when you're use to eating with your mate, eating alone reminds you that you're alone, that there's no one to carry on conversation about what happened that day. I found myself going to a restaurant just to be around other people. I didn't feel so all alone even if I was just drinking a cup of coffee among strangers.

→ *Consider...*

1. Identify foods that taste good to you and make you feel the way you want to feel.
2. Plan your meals.
3. When in a restaurant, sit at the counter so it's easier to talk to others.
4. Invest in a new cookbook, and prepare some new dishes. Join a gourmet club, and socialize with people who like food. You're likely to meet some very nice people, too.

I Know They're a Little Big for Me, But He Wore Them

For weeks after Rick died, I slept in his pajamas. I wouldn't change the sheets. I didn't want to wash away his sheer essence. I wanted to leave everything like it was when he was here. Sleeping in his pajamas was my secret. I was afraid to tell anyone about what I was doing, afraid they'd think I was crazy. During first year, I would think about Rick and the last time we did something together or the last time I went there, Rick was alive. The first anniversary of the death was so hard. I found myself catapulted right back to the event that changed my life forever.

→ *Consider…*

1. It's no secret that widows want to hold on to any physical evidence that their mates really existed. Believe me, you're not crazy! Every widow we've spoken to does this. It's normal!

2. Recognize that holding on to his essence, to his physical belongings, is part of the process of letting go. Give yourself permission to hold on to the physical as symbols of your closeness.

3. Buy something new to replace those things that belonged to him. How about some sexy pajamas? Or some satin sheets?

4. Some day you'll go to put on his pajamas and realize that you don't experience the same feelings or need that you had before. This is a good thing! It's a signal that you're moving forward.

I'm So Lonesome I Could…

Going home to an empty house gave me such an empty feeling. I talked out loud just to hear noise in the house. I had imaginary conversations with Rick, asking over and over, *Why? Why? Why?* Of course there was no answer. As time moved on, I would ask him what he thought about everyday things. I'd consult him before making any decision. It wasn't the same as him being with me, but it helped me feel like he was there. I didn't like being alone…life as I had known it dissipated in such a quick instant. The emptiness of the house was a constant reminder of a life I no longer had. Yes, being alone gave me time to reflect, time to plan, time to imagine, time to create a new life...aloneness was a bummer. Over time I found solace in being alone so I could listen to my inner voice. I'd speak out loud and listen to the sound of my own voice, finding comfort in simple ways.

→ *Consider...*

1. Leave the radio and a light on so that when you enter your home it's never dark or silent.

2. Write letters to yourself, and mail them. Your letters can be happy, sad, and anything in between. Your thoughts and feelings are what really matter. Delight in picking up and reading mail that you wrote just for you.

3. Get out of your funk. What are you doing to help others? What are your talents? What organization could use them? What kind of community service are you performing? Volunteer to help someone else.

4. Get a job. It could be part-time or full time. It could even be a job share. Hey, my two-day a week job in a designer showroom gives me a little extra cash, an opportunity to bring joy to others as they brighten up their homes, and the free time I want to spend with my family, friends, and myself.

Monday Nights at The Pit

For as long as I can remember, Rick and I ate dinner with our friends every Monday night at The Pit. Same day. Same time. Same place. Imagine my surprise when I show up for dinner after Rick's death and our friends never arrive. It's strange to me that I didn't hear from them again.

→ *Consider…*

1. When friends are a 'No Show,' follow up with them to understand what's going on. Don't let your hurt and assumptions interfere with your relationships.

2. Couples often feel awkward when one of the other couple has died. Query them. Honor their awkward feelings, bless them, and move on. Be grateful for the time you had together.

3. Refrain from believing you caused your friends to separate from you. They have their own issues they're dealing with...that have nothing to do with you.

Feed Her to the Lions…Quick

Before Rick died, my mother and I had planned a mother-daughter dream trip to Africa. Instead of canceling it, we decided to go even though it was only two weeks after Rick has passed on. Mother was swallowed up by grief, grief for her own husband and for mine. I was still in shock, and I needed comfort, the kind of comfort that a mother gives a daughter. My mother was expecting comfort from me. We were in conflict—neither of us could help the other out and both of us needed each other. Mother complained, was irritable, and nothing would please her. There was another mother-daughter pair on the trip. Mother wanted to know why I didn't respect her like the other woman's daughter did. Mother was behaving so badly, I wanted to put a slice of baloney in her pocket and feed her to the lions. And, given the opportunity, I just might have given her a little push and yelled, 'Have at her.' Fortunately, a widower on the trip rescued my mother by capturing my attention. We stayed up all night sharing our experiences. (Please do forgive me, Mama. I'm ever grateful that you weren't a Lion lunch!)

→ *Consider...*

1. Be patient! Patience is a lot more than a virtue; it's a survival tool. Patience has helped many relationships survive conflicts, hurt feelings, and misunderstandings. Rick used to voice the old sentiment, "Walk in the other guy's shoes for a while, then see how you feel." Well?

2. Recognize that others are hurting, too, because of the death. There's no one right way to grieve. We all grieve in our own way, in our own time.

3. Old patterns of behavior won't be repeated, so let go of your unrealistic expectations. Situations and relationships create a unique life of their own. View each experience as a new opportunity to learn something about others and yourself.

Mr. Charlie's Dip Stick

Another trip we had scheduled before Rick died was a family reunion in Georgia with his father's side of the family. In June of the year of his death, I went to the reunion alone and was fully embraced by his family. I felt wonderful and knew Rick would be pleased that I'd carried out our commitment to go. During the festivities, I met a distant relative, Mr. Charlie. He was a charming older man who had a delightful sense of humor. As is my custom, I asked for a hug, to which he quickly responded by embracing me with a big bear hug. My words to him, "You must always hug the widows, Mr. Charlie, because they are a quart low on hugs." Without missing a beat, he replied, "I'd love to check darling, but my dip stick is broke!"

→ *Consider…*

1. Unleash your sense of humor. It's one of those saving graces in life.

2. Laugh whenever you feel like it. Whereas you want to be sensitive to others, if it feels right, laugh. And, don't be concerned whether or not it's appropriate.

3. Ask for what you need and want. If you don't, others can't help you. Contrary to what might be popular opinion, most of us aren't mind readers. Don't expect others to anticipate and fulfill your needs.

Snuggle with the One You're With

If you've always slept with another person, trying to sleep without him is a challenge. The warm weight, the sounds of his sleeping, without the snoring, thank you, creates a lulling nocturnal rhythm that you miss when it's absent.

I was interviewing a nice gentleman for the book I was researching on widowers, who was still suffering from the loss of his wife three years before. We were sitting on the sofa in his living room and he asked me what I missed most about my husband. I told him it was the snuggling at night. He said he'd sleep beside me if doing so would help. So he held me in his arms as we lay down together for an hour or so. I could tell it fulfilled a need for him, too. We were like ships passing in the night. I thanked him for his kindness and told him he would be in the book…and so he is. Yes, he could have been an ax murderer, as Susan would suggest, but fortunately he wasn't…because I lived to tell the story. It was a foolish thing to do. I must have been really 'hungry' to take such a risk. Loneliness and desperation cloud our sense of self-protection. If you need closeness, find a way to fulfill the need.

➜ *Consider…*

1. Get a body pillow, one of the long ones you can throw your legs over. The pillow gets warm when it's under the blankets, and you almost feel like someone is in the bed with you.

2. Play soft music as you drift off to sleep.

3. Sleep in a different room, or even on the sofa for a while, until you get used to sleeping alone.

4. Snuggle up with an old-fashioned teddy bear. You can tell him your troubles. He'll never say, "Be strong" or "This will pass."

5. Sleep in your husband's pajamas. Doing so will make you feel close to him. I sure did!

6. Buy or knit a cozy blanket. Feel the luxury of wrapping yourself up snug and warm.

Rick's Teeth Sink Deep Into the Sea

During a very severe epileptic seizure, my darling, Rick, broke his upper jaw. He had to have his upper teeth replaced with a denture. I told him when he got it that I never wanted to see him without it…and I never did. When he died in the shower that morning, he must have had his denture out. Because we didn't see him in the morgue, we didn't know. Many weeks later when I was going through his personal care things, I came face to face with the denture. Well, what do you do with such a personal item? I couldn't bring myself to throw it in the trash. I didn't want to keep it. What would I do with it…pass it on to my children as an heirloom? Since we'd scattered his ashes at sea, I took the denture down to the Berkeley pier and threw it into the same sea that swallowed his ashes. When I think about some fisherman reeling in the denture, thinking there's a fish on the line, I laugh right out loud.

→ *Consider…*

1. Use your creativity when it's time to discard some of your husband's very personal items. Let yourself think outrageously, then you'll find the right way to do what you need to do.

2. Sorrow and humor are closely aligned. Things that are funny now were likely painful in the past. You may engage in some strange behaviors…and that's OK. Make a joke and share with others who can share in your ability to laugh at yourself and at less than favorable circumstances.

My Skin's Hungry…Can You Feed Me?

When you're used to being held by the one you love, by the one who has been by your side for so many years, you find that your skin hungers for human touch, for human closeness. When Rick was around, I liked to slide under his arm, put my arm around him, hold his hand. I love the human touch. My hunger for touch made me react in strange ways. One day I was pumping gas and engaging in conversation with a very nice older man. As our conversation came to a close, I said, "I'm a widow. Could you spare a hug?" I really made my remark in jest; however, his reaction was delightful. He responded, "Sure can, happy to oblige." Boy, did I feel gooood!

→ *Consider…*

1. Find a volunteer job that involves touching people, like at a rest home or children's center.

2. Ask your friends for physical closeness, like a hug or holding your hand. Be frank with them about missing human touch.

3. Treat yourself to a massage with a therapist you trust. Let the touch of their skin on yours soak in. Hmmmm!

4. Give blood. You'll feel good that you've done something good for a stranger.

I'm Not in Kansas, er, Oakland Anymore

Ann, my dearest friend, lives in San Diego, so I decided I wanted to move there. I wanted to be close to her and take some of the pressure off of Susan at the same time. I thought it would be fun to be close to Ann and her Marine General husband because we'd been through thick and thick and thin together. And, I realized I had become very dependent on Susan. So, Susan and I packed my bags and my car, and we drove south. Susan commented that she felt like she was driving her daughter to college and helping her move into the dorm.

My living in San Diego didn't work out. I was looking for a place to call home and realized I wouldn't find it there. I was terribly unhappy. I was as lonesome as I have ever been. Feeling reticent and almost ashamed, I called Susan and told her I wanted to come home. Well, Susan wanted me to live in Pacific Grove so she could keep an eye on me. You've already read what a disaster that was. Then I moved to Oakland to take care of my mother. I was searching for a place to call my own. I was searching for a home.

→ *Consider…*

1. It's OK to experiment and make mistakes. Take actions that seem right even if others don't approve of them. Recognize that learning often comes as a result of doing something that turns out to be wrong. You know that feeling…like when you said "Yes" to that guy at the school dance and when he offered his sweaty palm, you knew he was the wrong one for you. Once you realize you've made a mistake, own it, then move on.

2. Find a home where you feel comfortable and safe. Allow yourself to explore creative living arrangements, like sharing your home, trading it for a smaller one, moving into a condo in a gated community,

3. Check out the equity in your home. It's likely to be your largest asset. Is it working for you?

The Sink's Stopped Up

Rick and I took care of separate responsibilities. Rick took care of the mechanical things, like cars, plumbing, and dead pets. Now, I do realize that dead pets are not necessarily mechanical, however, disposing of them was his job. I took care of the bills, the groceries, and other womanly chores. You have to remember we were married way before the days of women's liberation. If I had gone first, Rick wouldn't have had a clue as to what to do with the bills. I'm relatively certain he could have made his way to the grocery store. One day when I was leaving for work I was at a total loss because the car wouldn't start. And wouldn't you know? On the very same day, I blew a fuse in the kitchen, and the sink stopped up. Where's my man when I really need him?

→ *Consider...*

1. Create a tool kit for yourself. Ask one of the clerks at the local hardware store for advice on what things you need for simple repairs.

2. Take a class at a local community college. You might be surprised at what you'll learn or who you'll meet.

3. Call the friends who have offered to help you. Tell them you need a fix!

4. Ask your neighbors for a referral, someone who's done good work for them.

5. Call on a younger relative with whom you can build or fortify a relationship. Consider nieces, nephews, grandchildren, and cousins.

Hanging on to the Last Thread of His Physical Existence

After 15 years, I finally gave away Rick's Pendleton robe. It was one that I'd given to him one Christmas. He loved it...and so did I. For a couple of years after Rick died, I wore it at night when I felt cold and lonely. Wearing it made me feel good. Then I put it away with some of his other clothing, like his sweaters and a pair of well-worn slippers, in a box. Every time I moved, the box went with me.

After so many years it seemed foolish for his clothes to take up space, so I decided to give them away. The robe was threadbare, not really fit for anyone to wear. I put it on top of a box of clothes I was giving to a women's shelter. I folded it gently and a tear of farewell trickled down my face. My last physical connection with Rick was severed. It was clearly up to me that I needed to fully embrace my new life.

→ *Consider…*

1. The physical things we hold on to are symbols of the emotional healing that still needs to take place.

2. Recognize that your connection to your mate will last forever.

3. Know that when you let the 'things' go, you acknowledge and bless your loved one and the memories you hold dear.

We're Just Friends…Really

Warren Mooney came along at just the right time in Mom's life. She had tried dating strangers with little success. Here was a man she had gone to high school with. They reconnected at a class reunion she heard about after she had moved back to Oakland. Mooney was divorced and very excited about seeing her again after all the years. She was "the girl that got away" to him. She's even said she might have married him if she had not met my dad at the YWCA dance that night. Mooney told her he felt he had lost his one true love when she married Rick.

Mooney was a very successful businessman and highly respected. He was very generous with contributions to community organizations and gifts to his friends and family members. He would pick Mom up in limos and take her to Trader Vic's and other fancy places in San Francisco. This lifestyle was new to her…and it was quite a treat! She spent money on nicer clothes and enjoyed being the woman on Warren Mooney's arm at classy events.

Mooney worshipped Mom. She couldn't understand why he hadn't made any sexual advances toward her. I suggested that he probably wanted to keep her on the pedestal she'd been on in his mind all these years and was afraid that sex might spoil their relationship. After all, he'd been married and divorced three times. She wanted him to know she was available and interested, so she bought a set of beautiful sheets and left them on his front porch. The note read, "In case of an emergency, break the seal, and call me."

Mooney was a wonderful, no-nonsense kind of fellow. He never mentioned the sheets. Once Mom asked him, "Warren, would you ever think of marrying me?' He answered swiftly, "Hell no, now eat you dinner, and let's get out of here."

Although they never 'got between the sheets,' having Mooney in her life was the perfect transition for her. He was a dear loving friend that she misses now that he's passed on.

➜ *Consider…*

1. Look up old friends and renew associations with them. Be open to the changes both of you have experienced. Don't get stuck in how they or things used to be or should be now.

2. Enjoy your dates. Refrain from looking at every man you date as a potential husband.

3. Invite a guy out on a date. Pick something you want to do and ask someone you think you'd enjoy getting to know better to go along with you. Your options are limitless...movie, concert, theatre, art show, ice cream... (Thank you, Women's Lib!)

Taking My Life Back

When I left Pacific Grove, I moved in with my mother in Oakland. She was in the early stages of Alzheimer's. She was not the vibrant woman she had once been. In many families the widowed daughter is the one to care for an older relative. I was here, and my sister was hundreds of miles away. So, by default, I was chosen to care for my mother.

I'm so thankful for my mother's friend, Beulah. Beulah was a 5'2" charming little lady, always ready to go. She had a wonderful sense of humor and a deep love for my mom. As Mom sunk deeper and deeper into Alzheimer's, my life became more and more difficult. These were stressful and difficult times. I had no time for a life of my own. Mom needed round-the-clock care. God bless Beulah. She was there for me. She helped me make the tough decision that Mom needed more care than I could give her. My friends agreed, acknowledging that she had lived a wonderful life and that I needed to move on with mine. I found a safe place where she could receive 24-hour care. It was so sad to see her waste away. However, I knew if I was to find a new life for myself, I had to let my mother go. I did. Not too long ago she passed on peacefully in the night.

→ *Consider…*

1. Participate in a caregivers' support group. Doing so will remind you that others are experiencing many of the same dilemmas you're facing. They're likely to have some good ideas that will be helpful to you.

2. Pace yourself. Take the time you need to get your own needs met. Don't put your life on hold.

3. Ask for the help you need from your children, neighbors, her friends, and professionals. Use respite care that's available from community organizations.

4. Forgive yourself for the tough decisions you may make. Do what you have to do—what's best for others AND what's best for you. Rejoice in your decisions.

Leave Me Alone…I'm in My Cocoon and I Like It Here

Prior to Mom's and my separation, I had had no time for grieving. With her back in Oakland, I could start dealing with the loss of my dad. At first I was angry. I really wanted to know WHY he left me and WHERE he went. I went for long walks in the forest near my home and spent days at Big Sur thinking, walking, and writing. I wanted to be alone. I wanted to think and read and work things out for myself. I was like a caterpillar, weaving the threads of a nice warm covering for the transformation. I distanced myself from the world, my husband, and friends. From the outside, cocoons feel crusty and hard if you try to touch them. It's not possible to see inside. From the inside of my cocoon, I could see out and chose the times to interact with others. In my search for answers, I read 75 books on religion, spirituality, reincarnation, and other topics helping me to prove that Dad was somewhere. I wanted to communicate with him or even better, hear his voice. On a day when I was most certainly at my lowest point, I felt his presence. I was comforted as I realized that he would always be just a breath away whenever I wanted him.

My husband kept a close watch, from a safe distance. I am so grateful for his love and patience. Here's a man, an only child, who had lost his own mother only a year before. He was dealing with his dad's loneliness and grief as well as his own. But he was always there for me. He was ever gentle and loving, even when he was puzzled by my silence or the crazy assortment of books I was reading.

Nature teaches that a butterfly cannot emerge from a cocoon until fully mature and complete. Each day the cocoon gets thicker and tougher in the beginning. It keeps the curious away and frustrates the loved ones who are trying to see inside. It is warm, dark, and safe, and there's room for only one caterpillar.

➔ *Consider...*

1. Recognize that cocooning is part of your own healing process.
2. Explain to your loving friends that you need to be alone and that your actions are not intended as an affront to your

relationship. Ask them to give you the space you need and to refrain from taking offense. Let them know you'll be more sociable as you work through your grief.

3. Write letters to your husband, expressing what it's like to live life alone. Keep the letters in a book or burn them, whichever feels right for you. Write letters to your mother or other relatives impacted by the death, expressing what couldn't be said in person. Write letters to dear friends and companions, expressing what you can't communicate verbally. Letter writing is a very effective cathartic experience. Send the letters if doing so increases understanding and enhances your relationships. It's quite acceptable to write a letter and not send it…sometimes it's better that way.

4. Read whatever books or articles you can find about life after death. It helps to know that humans have been searching for the same answers you're seeking for thousands of years. There's no one answer.

5. Talk about your questions, fears, and feelings with a spiritual leader or counselor.

6. Take a course at a local community college in philosophy or religious history. You'll have the opportunity to interact with other people of various ages and perspectives and hear different points of view.

7. Get a life coach so you can have support as you plan the rest of your life.

8. The answers to our questions about life are inside us. Allow yourself time to seek, listen, and accept your own process.

Chapter 6
Walking in the Present

Our thoughts were in the past—how life used to be. Our thoughts were in the future—what life would have been like. It's a challenge to stay in the present. Grieving is in the present. It's a reality we want to avoid…being in the present is much too painful. We want to escape. We want to be spared the agony of letting go of the one we love. We want to be protected from the ambiguity of an unknown future. To avoid reality, we keep busy—go back to work, volunteer our time— serving others. Yet, every waking moment is filled with memories of the lost loved one or musings about the future without them. There's great power in consciously choosing to stay in the present moment. The present is full of surprises, simple pleasures, chance meetings, the beauty of nature, and random acts of kindness. We must be present to notice and experience them. Walking in the present begins with a single step. So take that step with confidence.

Hello, Daughter, I'm Your Mother

The thing that pleases me the most about my new life, other than Manny being in it, is the wonderful relationship I have found with my daughter. Besides this project, we have done other things together that fill my heart with joy. I see in her the way I was with my mom before she lost herself to the terrible Alzheimer's disease. I remember what my own mom used to say when people chided her about not having a boy. She used the old quote, "A son is a son until he has a wife, but a daughter is a daughter all of her life." I regret that my other daughter is so far away and that I've never developed a close relationship with her.

Tragedy rendered a beautiful result. My relationship with Susan has made me look at the one with my own mother from a very different perspective. Mothers and daughters seem to have such a hard time creating their own identity, maintaining autonomy, and appreciating the gift of one another.

→ *Consider...*

1. Count your blessings...and name them one by one. Let others know how they've brought blessings into your life.
2. Tell your children and your friends that you love them.
3. Tell others what you want them to remember about you when you've moved on.
4. Write a letter for your children and close friends to be opened after you're gone.

Removing the Wedding Ring

One afternoon, I was sitting alone by the window. I looked at my hands. They were a married woman's hands, complete with a wide antique gold ban on the third finger of the left hand. It was the ring I bought 25 years earlier to replace my original wedding band. I removed the wedding band and noticed the misshapen finger. It seemed no other ring would fit. Taking the band off was traumatic for me. It felt like a betrayal, like I was saying our life together didn't exist. I had a jeweler attach both Rick's and my wedding bands on my gold charm bracelet. The bracelet is beautiful, reminding me of all the wonderful years we wore the rings and what those years mean to me.

After an influx of insurance money for a robbery in my home, I purchased a new ring to replace the wedding band. I wore it with great pride long before I met Manny, knowing it was the ring I wanted to be my wedding band if I were to marry again. It's the wedding band I wear today.

→ *Consider…*

1. Create a ceremony to remove your ring. Honor the marriage and release your attachment to it so you can move forward in life.
2. Give the wedding ring to a member of the family who will cherish it as you have.
3. Spend money on yourself. Taking care of yourself is an important step in moving from grief to joy.

Table for One?

Table for one? Yeah, do you see anyone else with me? The host glared at me. She showed me to a table next to the kitchen door. I noticed a table for two at the window, so I said, "I'd like to sit at that table by the window." She huffed and walked me over to the table by the window. It was obvious she didn't like doing so one bit. You see, no one expects to get a satisfactory tip from a 'little old lady' so they don't want her taking up a good table. Although married women eat in restaurants every day without their mates, when you're a widow, hearing *table for one?* is like the fingernails scraping the chalkboard. Maybe it's you. Maybe it's the host. Maybe it's the situation. Anyway, when you eat out alone, consider it a good opportunity to use those assertive skills.

→ *Consider...*

1. Invite a friend over to eat with you.

2. Meet someone in a restaurant for lunch or dinner.

3. Meet someone for breakfast. It's a great meal to eat out and gets your day off to an early start. Lots of small coffee shops get to know you, and the staff make you feel special when you visit.

4. Plan a dinner party. Invite a variety of people who don't know each other. See what chemistry is created.

I'm a Widow, Not a Divorcee

Mom told everyone she met she was a widow. She felt that being single due to the death of her mate was much more dignified than being divorced. And she has always been a classy lady. It was important for people to know that she had been happily and proudly married to a wonderful man for more than 39 years who took off for Heaven unexpectedly.

When Mom and Dad had disagreements in the early days of their marriage, Mom used to threaten to divorce him. His answer was always the same, "We can't afford it!" So they teased one another that poverty kept them together.

→ *Consider...*

1. Realize that when you tell people you're a widow, you're paying tribute to you partner.

2. Be proud of your marriage. Talk about it. It's OK to tell others about this important time in your life. Be aware of who's around when you're talking. If other widows are in the room, be sensitive to their situations and use discretion.

3. Be proud of the 'good relationship' credit you've built up as a married lady. Your good 'credit' demonstrates you've been a faithful friend and lover to one man for the time you were married. Realize you're starting a new account with this new life.

I'd Like to Get to Know You...Maybe

I decided one way to meet eligible men was to advertise in the newspaper. And, I decided widowers would make a good target market. After all, they knew what it was like to lose a partner. So I put an ad in the paper saying, *Widowers over 60 are wanted for interviews for a book.* Well, the typesetter put in *6'* instead of *60*. I didn't realize this until one of the interviewees said he was curious why the men I was interviewing had to be over 6 feet tall! I decided to

46

let the ad run as it was since I like tall men. After completing my formal interview, I'd give the guy my number and suggest we meet for coffee…if I liked him. If I didn't like the guy, I'd thank him for his help and tell him he'd be in the book.

→ *Consider…*

1. Meet new people doing things you like to do or want to learn how to do. Join a bird watching group. Take a class. Join a religious organization. Sing in the choir. Learn how to play a new sport. Join a fan club. Take dancing lessons. These are just a few ideas…think out of the norm!

2. Get a job where you'll see lots of people.

3. Volunteer for a community project, like a community garden or beach clean up. How about being a bell ringer for The Salvation Army at Christmastime? Now that's a wonderful way to meet all kinds of people.

Branded for Life

When I was in the depth of despair, I needed something to remind me that I had a new life. The man across the street has some beautiful butterfly tattoos on his shoulder, not your average tattoo, especially for a big hulky man named Joe. By asking him lots of questions, I learned about the famous tattoo artist in San Francisco who created his tattoos. The more I thought about it, the more I liked the idea of a 'new life reminder'—a butterfly seemed to fit my need. Now, I'm a very conventional lady, well, sort of—and the thought of having a tattoo anywhere it could be seen was a complete turn off. But, placing it where I could only see it intrigued me. I contacted the artist, found out how much it would cost, and decided to treat myself. Anyone who tells you tattooing doesn't hurt like hell is crazy. My small, pretty tattoo of a butterfly is on my hip. How did I know I'd be visiting a naturist resort where there are no secrets? The butterfly reminds me that each day is the beginning of a new life.

➔ *Consider…*

1. Set a goal. Determine something you want to accomplish.
2. Create reminders of your goals and put them where you can see them. Make posters, scrapbooks, and pictures. Use bulletin boards, your refrigerator door, the bathroom mirror, a calendar, and Post-it notes to display your goals.
3. Create symbols that represent your new life. You don't have to have them tattooed on your body! As for me, the butterfly represented the promise of a new life, the promise that the metamorphosis I was going through would yield a new beginning.

Mustering the Courage to Step Out…on Her Own

Mom didn't take to new situations easily like you might think she would. When she decided she'd go to a singles group function for the first time, she had to muster all her strength to get dressed and drive to the church. Then she sat crying in the car for 10 minutes, thinking how awful it was going to be to walk alone into a room full of strangers. You see she'd always loved walking into a room on Dad's arm. He was always the tallest and best-looking man in the room, and she was oh so proud to be with him. Mom finally got the courage to get out of the car and walk up to the door. Half way into the room, she turned in fear and ran back to the car. She did try again and was successful. She had a good time and met some nice men who wanted to dance with her which made all of her efforts worthwhile. For certain, that first time was very difficult, more difficult than she expected.

➔ *Consider…*

1. Compare stepping out to going to the dentist. It's necessary if you want to move on with your life, just like going to the dentist helps you keep your own teeth.

2. Take scary things a little at a time. Limit the time you spend in a difficult and uncomfortable situation. Increase the time in that environment as you feel more comfortable in it.

3. Keep in mind that "By this time tomorrow, it will be all over." Don't say this too often to yourself, however; you don't want to scare your life away.

4. Reward yourself—a hot bubble bath, new earrings, a pedicure—for doing something when you feel really uncomfortable.

Did She or Didn't She? Who Cares?

When Mom moved back to Oakland to take care of Granny, she met a hairdresser named Joann at the church where she attended the singles group. Joann was fun and bubbly and they became girlfriends—like the ones you have as teenagers. Joann, who was having challenges with her mother, needed a mother substitute. And, Mom needed a daughter substitute since we were on the outs. Joann's friendship was just what Mom needed to feel young again and to regain her self confidence. Joann went with Mom when she had her facelift—the one to make her look and feel better, not younger. Then, Joann encouraged Mom to become a blond, promising that blondes really did have more fun. Mom looked great! And, she found out that blondes do have lots of fun. Granny, Mom's mom, initially told her she looked like a 'woman of the streets,' but later complimented her on her new look. Mom was ready for the dating game! Mom and Joann had good times together. Then it was time for them to part. This temporary relationship helped Mom take another step out of her loneliness and into independence.

→ *Consider…*

1. Find friends with compatible needs so you can help each other out.

2. Recognize that people come in and out of your life when growth is required. You can learn from them or get trapped.

3. Know when to let go of relationships that are no longer balanced or mutually valuable.

Mr. Goodbar's Not Out There, is He?

Dating! Bah Humbug! It was really hard to get out in the dating world. I was out of practice. Heck, I never had any practice. I was married all my life.

As Susan just mentioned, I attended a church singles group in Orinda. It was a good place to dance, socialize, and meet some very nice gentlemen. I even went out with some of them. Being in a group was helpful and dancing is a way to get close to men and satisfy that skin hunger. Many of the people in this group were divorced and liked the single life. In retrospect, I was looking at every man as a potential husband. I wanted to be married because that was my lifestyle. I was so lonely that I hurt. This experience fulfilled a need for a while, and then I moved on.

→ *Consider…*

1. Never devalue yourself. Don't be in search of the elusive right man for you. Be yourself, and let the men find you.
2. Don't let yourself feel desperate. Hear yourself saying, "I wouldn't marry this man if he was the last one on Earth" and mean it!

Knowing When to Move on Because Barbie's Still in the House

Ken was one of the widowers I interviewed for my book. After the interview, I gave him my number and told him he could call me if he wanted, which he did. That call started what I hoped would be a long-term committed relationship. I was gung ho, ready to move on. The more I learned about Ken, the more I realized he wasn't ready for a relationship. Barbie had been dead for two years and her cosmetics were still in the bathroom. Next!

→ *Consider...*

1. Like the plague, avoid men who are still living in the past.

2. Talking about memories is wonderful and sometimes appropriate. When his former life is all he can talk about, it's your signal to move on. Let him get over it on his own.

3. When considering remarriage, think long and hard about it. Expose any ghosts floating around <u>before</u> you say, "I do."

I'm No Nurse with a Purse

As you might imagine or may have experienced for yourself, I became quite frustrated with the dating scene. More than sex, many of these guys were looking for a rich woman to take care of them. Can you believe it? Well, I was neither rich nor interested in being a nursemaid. There was nothing for me in that kind of relationship. These freeloaders were shysters of a different sort, but no better than the contractors and service people who charge widows more for their services. Widows are taken advantage of daily—charged for services that aren't performed or that have been completed in a shoddy fashion. Widows, whose husbands use to take care of these kinds of things, are prime targets for the unscrupulous. Don't get taken!

→ *Consider...*

1. Walk, no, RUN away from any man who's after your money!

2. Seek out professional advice on how to take care of the money you do have.

3. Share your decisions about money with someone you trust.

4. Look at every bill and restaurant check to make sure you've been charged the correct amount.

5. Keep track of your spending so you're a confident, wise money manager.

Looking for Love on 101

Driving from San Diego to Oakland one sunny day, a trip I took often to visit Ann and Ed, I noticed a handsome man in a dark sedan. We passed one another, passed again, smiled, and waved. We were playing tag. When I realized I needed a cup of coffee to stay alert, I decided to stop at the Apple Farm, a delightful place right off of Highway 101 in San Luis Obispo. As I entered the parking lot, I noticed that handsome man in the dark sedan pulled in beside me. We smiled and laughed as we got out of our cars. He offered to buy me that cup of coffee. When we had finished our coffee, we went to our cars, and he gave me a big lip lock kiss. Hmmm...it tasted goooood.

Ships passing in the night again. Nice things can happen if you let them. I know, Susan, he, too, could have been an ax murderer, but he wasn't.

→ *Consider…*

1. Expect to meet new friends in unusual places.

2. Smile and say "Hello" when you meet new people. Most people can't resist returning a smile. Practice smiling at frowny people and see what happens.

3. Keep music in your head. I've got music playing in my head most of the time. Anybody can tell because I'm a hummer. My humming brings on attention and usually the comment, "You must be happy." And, that I am. How could I not be with music dancing inside my heart and soul?

Everything You Wanted to Know About Sex…and Orgasms

One day, seemingly out of the blue, Mom called. She wanted to know how to handle the "sex thing." She said, "These men want sex. What should I do?" Can you imagine having this conversation with your mom? Well, I told her I really couldn't advise her except to tell her if she felt comfortable having sex, then why not? I told her to be safe, use condoms, and follow her gut feeling. I didn't want her to end up with a sexually transmitted disease or with that ax murderer. You see, this was obviously new territory for Mom. She and Dad had been married for so many years that sex wasn't a big part of their life. They enjoyed the closeness and tender feelings that come with long-term loving relationships, but not the sex act per se.

A few weeks later, Mom called again. She exclaimed, "Wow, this sex thing is great! How come you never told me about orgasms?" Watching my own mother go through teenage pubescence was fun. She became the epitome of defining oneself. Life was truly unfolding anew for her.

→ *Consider…*

1. Expect excitement and strong feelings when you're in bed with a man.
2. Be certain that having sex with a man is your choice and that you're not feeling pressured to do so.
3. Think of sex as play; don't take it so seriously.
4. Practice safe sex no matter what your age.
5. Know that sex is a couple's unique matter, that sex with one man may not be like sex with another. Sure the mechanics are the same; however, if you expect sex with a new partner will be like it was with your husband, you're likely to be disappointed.
6. Relax and enjoy...EUREKA!

Clearing out the Clutter

When Rick was alive, the fridge reflected the activity in our lives. The clutter in the refrigerator continually reminded me that Rick was not here. Bits and pieces of leftovers. Eggs that had survived long past the expiration date. Bread that was stale. Rancid butter. Sour milk. Uneaten casseroles brought over by a dear soul. Leftovers. Why had he left me? I felt like a leftover.

→ *Consider...*

1. Clean out that clutter. Start with an easy area, like the linen closet. Don't forget the medicine chest—it's a repository for all kinds of stuff and all kinds of memories.
2. Don't save the leftovers from yesterday. Throw them out.
3. Clean out the memories that no longer serve you, that get in your way of moving on.
4. When you buy something new, make room for it by giving away the old. A new set of dishes can really light up the kitchen and your perspective.

Recycling Earthly Possessions

It took me a while before I could get around to giving Rick's things away. Fortunately I had good friends who helped me through the trauma. His clothes went to Phil, a friend, who was 6'4" like Rick. His model railroad was disassembled, with some of the trains going to my daughters, and the board going to a stranger. He had so many toys that it took a while to find homes for those possessions he enjoyed so much. I found that finding them new homes made space for other things and opportunities to come into my life. I kept a few of the HO trains for my grandchildren, who aren't old enough to really appreciate them yet. The right time for sharing this aspect of their grandfather will come, and I'll joyfully pass them along.

→ *Consider…*

1. Recognize we hold on to the tangible because we need the physical evidence that our mates were here at one time.

2. Pass his possessions along to your children and grandchildren. Ask them to pick out things that hold meaning for them.

3. Donate his things to shelters or charitable organizations.

4. Gift his friends with special items that will bring back good memories.

Celebrating the Holidays in a Different Way

You can choose to do something different at holiday time as Susan's friend did by going on a cruise. I highly recommend this. Holidays are some of the very worst times for widows, just ask one. Start new traditions. Your children may be dismayed by your decision. Remind them there are more than 300 other days in the year to get together. Let them tough it out.

→ *Consider…*

1. Don't sit at home and remember how it used to be. Don't make yourself miserable.

2. Work at a shelter. Servers are always needed during the holidays.

3. Visit residents in a rest home. They always need a personal touch.

4. Go on a trip. New sights and sounds help heal the hurt.

5. Encourage your children to experience the holidays in a different way with you. They can be persuaded.

I'll Take That Car

I wanted a new car, one that represented the new me. I went to the showroom with a good idea of what I wanted. I met a terrific salesman and sell, he did. He asked if I wanted to test drive the car...of course I did. Then he attached my personal license plates, BW HUGS, to the car. I bought the car without even asking how much it was. How could I resist! Susan almost died...she scolded me for buying something so expensive without knowing the price tag first.

→ *Consider...*

1. Join AAA or another auto club so you can get service if your car has a problem.

2. Get a cell phone so you can call for help when you need it.

3. Oh yes, do look at the price tag before you buy anything!

How the Hell's Angels Showed Me the Way

Driving around in the hills in my big Cadillac, I became completely lost. I was exploring my new surroundings. I saw some Hell's Angels motorcyclists, dressed in black leather and studs, stopped by the side of the road. Tired of being lost, I pulled up beside them, rolled down the window, and asked, "Where the heck am I?" The big guy replied, "Where do you want to be?" I let him know I was looking for Los Gatos. "Lady, you ain't even close" was his response. They very politely pointed me in the right direction. Stopping was a foolish thing to do—they could have easily taken advantage of this little ol' lady in the big Cadillac. Susan says I must have a guardian angel. Over the years, I've found that a smile and a positive expectation will get you through some difficult situations.

→ *Consider…*

1. If you're not sure where you're going, don't drive in places alone.

2. Get a map, and use it. Chart your course before you leave.

3. When you must, address any stranger with respect and confidence. Don't show you're weak or afraid…that's when they could take advantage of you.

I Didn't Know I was Robbing the Cradle…But I'd Do it Again!

When I first met Manny, I didn't really know how old he was. I figured he was about my age…you know, after a while, our bodies often misrepresent our chronological age. Young people look old. Old people are well-preserved. It was not until we went for our marriage license, where we had to present our birth certificates, that I learned Manny was 12 years younger than me. If I had known that he was so much younger, I would have never dated him. Man…think of what I would have missed!

➡ *Consider…*

1. Don't let age be a criterion for you friendships.
2. Let kindness and trust be the guidelines you follow.
3. Listen to your inner voice about what's right for you.
4. Embrace new things and new people in your life.

Good Night, Rick…I Mean Manny

There are times I call Manny, 'Rick,' and bless his heart, he says that's OK. He recognizes that Rick was an integral part of my life for 40 years, so he says he doesn't mind. One night, we'd turned off the light as we were preparing for sleep. I said, "Good night, Rick," as I've been accustomed to doing most of my life. Manny said so lovingly, "Do you want to say good night to me, too?"

➡ *Consider…*

1. Calling your new partner your former partner's name is common. It's not a sign of disrespect. If your partner is offended, talk about it with him to learn why it upsets him.
2. Talk with your potential husband about this highly possible slip before you marry. Reassure him that being with you puts him in a rare class—he's your beloved.
3. Forget the man who is really mad about you miscalling his name. He's bad news.

Widowhood? Hey, I'm Newly Wed

The greatest gift in my life is my wonderful husband. The reality of my mother's experience makes each moment with him more important than anything else in my life. We are "present" with each other as a matter of consciousness and habit. The "present" is unwrapped anew every morning of our lives because of a sudden death 16 years ago. You may be thinking, how morbid. Yet, this isn't so, for there's no little black cloud of worry hanging over us. We've talked about what will happen when death parts us. We recognize death is part of the whole reality of living. Our culture neatly puts death to the side, no one likes to talk about it. It's not a part of daily life. There's no way to avoid the pain of a lost loved one. Knowing that love creates memories everyday makes life sweeter.

→ *Consider...*

1. Awareness of the potential in every moment of your life makes you more willing to be spontaneous and joyful.

2. Consciously create new memories with family and friends that go along with your treasured ones, the ones from the past.

Chapter 7

Walking into the Future

December 26, 1998. *Do you, Barbara, take this man, Manny, to be your lawful wedded husband, to cherish and love for the rest of your life? Oh yes, I do.* My words were hardly understandable because I was crying so much. Now that I think of it, Manny didn't look too steady either.

During the wedding ceremony, I knew there was no going back to the past. The first time I married, I had no idea how my life would change. This time I knew full well that this was for the rest of my life. My decision was irreversible. The only direction I could move in was into the future, with a man who was the love of my life. How fortunate for me to have two true loves during my lifetime. Someone up there must surely be watching over me.

When we decided to get married, we wanted to be sure it would be a very private affair. Neither of us likes social events. We discussed the place, who we'd like to be there, and who would marry us. I just wanted someone to make it legal and ask God's blessing on us. So we decided that it would be best to be with Susan and Dick in their home. We asked their minister to perform the ceremony.

Susan created a gorgeous bouquet of sweet-smelling lavender roses. Dick was there for Manny to honor his new step father-in-law, who was ten years younger that he!

We were married in front of Susan and Dick's fireplace with the two of them to support us. Manny looked like my Prince Charming.

He didn't seem to mind that I felt like I looked fat. He vowed to love me forever. Aaaahhhhh!

Snickers, a wonderful pork roast, was the main event for the wedding feast. Susan had purchased Snickers at a Four-H auction during the summer. He was delicious, but it did seem strange eating something you know by its first name. Dinner, including a wedding cake, was great. Dick and Susan did their best to make the day special for us. And they did.

After the lovely ceremony, the dinner, and the warm loving "thank yous," we drove about six blocks to a nice motel in Pacific Grove. Our room was a couple's joy—a heart-shaped hot tub took center stage. Bigger than the bed, the hot tub sat idle. There were no handles, no steps, and no way we could get in it. We did give it some thought, and well, it's the thought that counts, right? Even though Manny and I had been living together for a couple of months, this night was different. It was special. We were husband and wife, and I felt fabulous.

I was a happily married lady again. While I was growing up, my Mom and Dad, who survived the Depression, told me to marry a man with a steady job. So I did again. I was glad that Manny went off to work every day. It gave me time to adjust to being part of a couple again and some cherished time for myself.

It was important to start our life together the way we wanted and not worry about anyone else. We suspected that we had likely hurt some feelings because his family wasn't invited to the wedding. Whatever discord we created dissipated. His children honored us with a round trip to Hawaii. Our dear friends, Ann and Ed, gave us a week in their timeshare there…so what could have been better?

Haven't I Been Here Before?

As a widow and even as a re-married widow, you'll have flashbacks, a time when you experience some of the same feelings you have had in your life with your former husband. It may happen when you hear certain music or smell his aftershave lotion.

Recently, I experienced a terrifying flashback. I was getting ready to go to Susan's house. Manny was standing at the door in his robe, planning to take a shower once I left. This was the same scenario on the day Rick died. I cried all the way to Susan's house I couldn't wait to call Manny to see that he was still alive. We always say, "I love you" when we part, acknowledging that it may be the last time we ever see each other. This could be a good reason for getting that cell phone…huh?

→ *Consider…*

1. Don't let flashbacks overwhelm you. Recognize them, bless your mate, and focus your attention on the good of the present.
2. Find new places to go with your new husband or companion. Go to new restaurants. Take up a new hobby.
3. Get help from a professional if the déjà vu experiences occur often, are troubling, or prevent you from moving on.

Initiating New Projects

When we were going through this process, we learned that there are lots of widows out there and that there are few somewhat unknown resources available. We learned that being a widower was better than being a widow, that friends and family felt compelled to take care of the widower, that the widow was left alone in her grief and longing.

We wanted to change this. We wanted to provide information and, more importantly, a guide for moving through the widow experience and emerging as a self-assured woman ready to live life anew.

➔ *Consider...*

1. Join an interest group and broaden your network of friends. Never be reluctant to share your status as a widow. Tell your story with pride and comfort someone else at the same time.

2. Write about your experience. Your words will provide comfort to you as well as others. Submit your stories to neighborhood newspapers. The editors are always looking for human interest stories. If you want to learn more about writing, join a writing group. Bookstores, junior colleges, and community schools are good sources for finding such groups.

3. Connect with other widows. When you start asking around, you'll be surprised to find many widows in your circle of friends and acquaintances. The more you inquire,

the more comfortable you'll become in asking others about their status. Invite them to your home. Participate in social events together. Some places to meet other widows include recreation centers, senior citizen groups, Parents Without Partners meetings, religious institutions, and coffee shops. You'll also meet widows and other wonderful people when you volunteer and participate in community activities.

Dream BIG Dreams...and Help Them Come True

When I was young, I wanted to be an actress. I longed to be before the lights. When I saw a movie, I would take on the persona of the heroine and play her out...until I saw the next movie. Over the years, I've enjoyed being on stage—working with volunteers, conducting workshops, speaking on behalf of organizations. I like sharing what I know and entertaining anyone who wants to be entertained. Rather than serving coffee and doughnuts on the docks, I really should have been part of the Bob Hope Road Show overseas. Now that would have been something!

Now, I want to take the joy of sharing and entertaining on the road to speak with others who have taken the journey from widowhood to self-assurance. I want to find out where your walk has taken you. I want to find out how your journey is unfolding. An unparalleled version of my dream is being revealed as we write these words. Excitement fills our hearts as we make plans to visit widows around our great country.

We also dream of creating a widow's support network around the world that provides support and information for women who have become widows. In Chapter 9, we'll share the details with you so you can form your own support group.

It seems like a good idea to share one of Manny's dreams. He wants to stand on the Great Wall of China. Now, I must admit this doesn't do a thing for me. However, his dream is his dream, and I love him. So guess who will be standing beside him on the Great Wall? You're right! I'll be there. I might even find that I'll enjoy the experience. Helping him realize one of his dreams will bring me much pleasure even if it's not one that I have for myself. I rejoice with him as he does with me when our dreams come true.

Although standing on the Great Wall isn't a shared dream, we do have some common ones. We want to visit all the presidential libraries and see all of our wonderful National Parks. We record our dreams in a 'wish' book, knowing full well that we'd have to live to be 200 to see all of them realized! Yet, dreaming keeps us all young at heart, and realizing our dreams brings us such delight.

➔ *Consider…*

    1. What are your dreams? What are you doing to make them come true? What will your regrets be when you look back on your life, realizing you didn't take necessary actions to help your dreams come true?

2. Make your dreams more real by sharing them with people who love and care about you, those who will encourage you to pursue them.

3. Keep a dream book. Write down your dreams. Identify any actions you can take to make those dreams come true. As your dreams are realized, mark them with the date. You might be surprised as the dreams you manifest enrich your life.

4. Help someone else realize his or her dreams. What joy you'll find in their joy.

5. None of us knows what the future holds. What prepares us for the unknown is an open mind, an accepting heart, a willingness to change—to create and go with the flow, and an enthusiasm for life. It's impossible to embrace the future when you're still holding on to the past.

Think forward.

Dream forward.

Plan forward.

Move forward.

Chapter 8

Walking Your Own Walk

Imagine...

Maybe in another universe with another sun, we're born again and have some iota of wisdom from our past lives. Maybe there's a place with never ending possibilities, a place where there would be no illness and no death. When you wanted to move on or were bored, you could just close your eyes and change. If you wanted to know what it's like to fly, you could change into a bird. If you wanted to sleep all winter, you'd change into a bear. If you wanted to swim in the deep blue sea, you'd become a whale.

In this universe, you can explore anything you wish, have anything you desire, or just relax. You can read all the books you ever wanted to read. There's no pressure to do anything. Your loved ones are not forgotten; it's joyful to remember them. You don't grow old. Your options are limitless. You're glad to be there. In this place of wonderment, the colors, smells, tastes, sounds, and emotions are intense.

Maybe it's sitting at the feet of the Master, hearing all the stories first hand, then being sent out to other worlds to spread the word. Can you imagine sitting, looking into God's eyes, feeling His hand upon you, knowing He speaks to you and holds you dear. Such imagination can boggle the mind.

Facing Fear & Moving Forward

I've found that there are times when I have an overwhelming fear that Manny will die, and I'll be left to face life alone again. Once I dreamed that Manny was dead. I kept hearing *Manny will never come home again*. I woke up crying and found Manny in the bed beside me. My fear is groundless, purely emotional.

Such fears are common. Many widows have adamantly stated they will never love again, never remarry because they don't want to experience the horrific loss again. I respect every woman's right to believe and feel what she wants; however I don't let the fact that people are killed in auto accidents keep me out of cars or the knowledge that airplanes crash keep me from flying. Life is uncertain. We take chances every day. We can chose to live in fear or we can face it, rejoicing that we have one more day to live.

Being left a widow is a terrible thing, but not the worst that can ever happen to you. It may be helpful to consider some of the things that are even worst than the death of a loved one. My mother's 10-year bout with Alzheimer's is a fate worse that death. I think about Superman, Christopher Reeve, and consider if I could face the challenges he faces every day. I think about parents who have buried their children. For me there is nothing worse than outliving your child. Think about those situations that would be worse than death for you and your loved ones.

Be realistic, and face your situation. Cull it into perspective. Give yourself some time, BUT, if you find that you're not getting on with life, take a hard look at what's getting in your way. Consider reading the historical accounts of the pioneer women that settled our country. They persevered against nature, men, and their own fears to create a place for us in history.

Read about conditions for women in other parts of the world. You'll find that your situation is far better than theirs. I praise God every day that I was born in America in an enlightened age. Examining the trials and tribulations of our sisters of the past and around the world will help you overcome your grief and get on with your life. Whether you are 20, 35, 40, 55, 60, or 70, you still have days to live and gifts to contribute.

And, Moving On

Count the times you've said to yourself or someone else, *Someday I'm going to....* Or perhaps you have said *I've always wanted to have this or that. Or when we get more money, I will do whatever.* Now's the time to act.

Things will never be the same. Your life has changed, and it can never be like it was, no matter what you do or say. Change is just that, nothing more, not good or bad, just changed, just different. The sooner you make peace with change, the sooner you're in a state of renewal.

Remember my first positive thought when I became a widow? I don't have to ask anyone about what I plan to do. I can...but I don't have to. I'm the master of my new life. So are you. If you want to take a trip around the world, you can. If you've always wanted a Coach handbag, a $100 perm, a massage, a facial, or even a tattoo, now is the time. Train ride? All aboard! Want company on this new journey? Seek out new and old friends.

Make plans to move on. Where there are problems, there are opportunities, there are solutions. You must be willing to acknowledge the situation you're in and be open to finding a solution that's satisfactory.

Would you take a trip with someone who suggests he or she doesn't have a clue as to where you're going and doesn't really care if you get anywhere? Widows need a plan. It could be as simple as how you're going to pay your bills. You may need to make a decision about keeping your home or moving into another. You're much more capable than you even think you are. Take me, for example, I was very capable of paying the bills, holding down a full time job, running the household, and taking care of my husband. There was no magic wand that tapped me on the shoulder to make me anything other than the person I was, the person I am. I just needed time to grieve and get on with my life. I was not and have never been a helpless female. Who has time? There's so much I want to do. So, even if you have been helpless in the past, you're really not. A plan is not a break in faith of the past. It's a promise that you'll have a future…which can be very bright…if you'll let you own light shine.

Chapter 9

Helping Others Walk Their Own Walk

Why do widows feel all alone when there are so many of us out there? Why don't widows share what we learn? Why don't widows offer comfort to other widows in a way that no others can? Why don't we look for ways to make the widow's journey a little less painful, a little less sorrowful, a little less desperate?

There may be many answers to these questions. We're caught up in our own grief. We don't think anyone else can understand the experience. We're in need of help and comfort. We want others to experience the hurt and pain we feel. We lose our will to live. We don't think we have anything to share. We feel helpless, hopeless, and lost.

It doesn't take but an instant to go back to the pain of becoming a widow. The emotion of that experience is easy to call up. We forget that our experiences are our teachers. We tend to forget about our responsibility to help others fully experience the grieving process as well as begin a new life. We realize that our focus, and rightfully so, has been on getting our own needs met and our own desires satisfied.

When your grief has subsided and the new journey has become fulfilling, it's time to give to others. For in our giving, we often receive exactly what is needed for our own healing. One of the reasons we exist is to share what we know with others, to help others along the way. We believe the privilege of helping other widows is a high calling.

Although my mother's friend, Beulah, suffered from asthma all her life, she was an inspiration to me. She had worked with Mom at the Department of Agriculture in Berkeley. When I think back, I can see that this little woman gently challenged me to muster up courage and gave me invaluable support when I was dealing with Mom's Alzheimer's. She set a wonderful example of how one widow can help another. She also epitomized what happens when you don't let your widowhood hold you back, when you let yourself get on with your life.

Beulah was a very young widow with a young daughter to raise. When her daughter married, Beulah did whatever she chose to do. She didn't let age, her medical condition, or her singleness get in her way. She traveled all over the world, collecting mementos of the wonderful times she enjoyed.

She recognized the onset of Alzheimer's in Mom. She reassured me when I was filled with guilt, acknowledging it was time to move on with my life. She did her best to placate Mom on our Africa trip…she concurred that we should throw Mom to the lions. Yes, Beulah was full of life, in spite of the many challenges she faced during her lifetime.

Beulah's gone now. I miss her so. The last time I saw her, I kissed her and told her to say 'hello' to Rick for me. I asked her to tell him that I never looked better or felt sexier. She chided me saying, "Shame on you," with a twinkle of knowing in her eye.

Thank you, Beulah, for being my role model. Because of the wit and wisdom you shared with me, I've been better able to deal with my own challenges.

You, too, can be a helper, role model, and mentor to other widows. Remember that your actions influence the actions of others. Just think…if you helped a widow, then she helped another, then that one helped another…then the state of widowhood wouldn't be nearly as lonely and painful as many of us have experienced.

Here are some of our suggestions for assisting other widows. Be creative. Certainly there are limitless ways to care for our sisters.

1. Seek out widows in the places you go, like your place of worship, a community group, or where you volunteer, and engage in conversation.
2. Host a Widows' Support Group. [See details below.]
3. Share your story with others to offer encouragement, hope, and strength when and where it's appropriate.
4. Visit widows—take a casserole, flowers, a keepsake, a book [like this one!] to comfort them.
5. Listen with your heart. Never tell another not to cry or grieve or that this is God's will. Your listening and empathetic responses will make a marked difference for this widow.
6. Write articles for your local paper about moving from widowhood to rebirth.
7. Express yourself in poetry, song, or visual arts. Share your expression with others.

8. Invite widows to your home for holidays.

9. Invite widows to participate in volunteer activities.

10. Provide emotional support without vicariously reliving your own experience.

11. Provide assistance to those who are likely to become widows because their mates are terminally ill.

12. Volunteer to work with the widows-to-be in a local hospice program.

13. Gift your widowed friend with a makeover. Enjoy a girls' day out.

14. Refer the widow to legitimate legal, financial, health, emotional, and spiritual services.

In providing assistance to widows, you must be sensitive to the timing of your efforts. Sometimes you need to wait. Sometimes you need to gently push. Sometimes you need to walk away because you're getting sucked into her despair and grief. Trust your intuition. You'll know exactly what to do.

We all learn by example. We're all role models, even if we don't want to be. We find comfort in knowing that another has survived a similar ordeal. Don't let others down. Don't fail to carry out your responsibility to your widowed sisters. What joy you'll find in sharing your success in uncovering a new life. What peace you'll feel as you emerge from your grief and exude a new enthusiasm for living. What satisfaction you'll receive by helping others to begin anew!

Suggestions for Hosting a Widows' Support Group

Group support for the journey of life is always helpful. Some people only need a group for a specific period of time whereas others will be a part of a group for a long period of time because of the relationships they develop. The purpose of forming a group is to support one another and provide accountability for the things you want to accomplish as individuals. Group members need to take responsibility for their participation and for encouraging each other to be faithful. All groups need guidelines to be effective. These suggestions provide some structure and process for your group. Use them as a discussion-starter. All members need to agree on the guidelines.

✓ **Participation**: Each member is encouraged to respond aloud to the day's questions or topics. Anyone may choose to "pass" or not speak at any time without explaining why. Members should take turns as the discussion leader.

✓ **Preparation**: Members prepare for meetings by reading or journaling about the topic agreed upon by the group.

✓ **Presence**: Members are present unless unforeseen circumstances prevent it. Any member unable to attend always communicates with another member.

✓ **Personal Focus**: Members talk about their own experiences rather than talking about others'. They refrain from giving advice.

✓ **Gentleness**: Members deal with one another kindly, always striving to understand and be understood.

✓ **Confidentiality**: What is shared in the group, stays in the group.

✓ **Meditation or Prayer**: Members spend time each day thinking or praying, soliciting strength and support for the group members as well as for oneself.

✓ **Structure:** Meetings need to have a dependable format and time limit. The member who agrees to be the discussion leader each week prepares a story or words of inspiration that presents a theme. Or group members can agree to "check in" at the beginning of each meeting and decide on the topic that seems most relevant in the present moment. Even a spontaneous discussion needs structure. Structure is very important to us human beings. We all need it, in varying degrees, especially when working together in a group. Through experimentation, your group will find the one that fits.

Suggested Agenda for Meeting

1. Open with a greeting, prayer, or brief meditation.
2. Introduce the meeting topic.
3. Discuss the topic, with each member participating as they feel moved to respond. (The leader encourages members to speak, but protects their right to "pass.")
4. Wrap up or summarize the conclusions and benefits of the discussion.
5. Agree on specific goals for the week ahead and suggested topic for next meeting.

6. End with a prayer or blessing that is ritualized—consistent for the ending of every meeting. An example is "Let us go forward with peace, joy, and love."

You can add time for silence or activities. As the host, be cognizant to the needs of each member. Recognize that some meetings will be great and others will be ordinary. Keep in mind that as individuals you may go away from a meeting feeling wonderful while others may feel sad. Also remember that some meetings will meet someone else's needs but not yours. Have realistic expectations and follow a plan of some kind for every meeting.

Some Questions & Answers about Hosting a Widows' Support Group

Q: Where do we find widows for our group?

A: *Widows are everywhere. Check with your friends, relatives, acquaintances, business associates. Advertise in the classified ads. Ask a newspaper reporter to write a story about you and the group you want to start.*

Q: Where do we meet?

A: *Meet in a free, comfortable, and safe place. This could be in a church, library, community center, or your home.*

Q: How often do we meet?

Barbara Whitman Gaeta and Susan Whitman

A: *This is entirely up to the group. You want to meet often enough to enhance the continuity of your relationships, but not so often that it interferes with other aspects of life.*

Q: How many widows should be in our group?

A: *This is entirely up to your group. If the group is too large, there won't be time for everyone's comments. If the group is too small, members may feel pressure to talk about their concerns when they don't really want to. Research tells us that groups between 5 and 8 are the most effective.*

Q: What do we do when others want to join?

A: *The group needs to make a decision about how members join and exit. Once the group has congealed, it's hard for a new person to enter and feel a part of the group. After all, the current members have history together. Your group might offer to sponsor a new widows' support group. Doing so would help a new group form using your support and wisdom while you keep your group in tact.*

Q: How formal should the meetings be?

A: *The level of formality ought to fit the group. Too much formality may put some of the members off. Too little may do the same thing. Work with your group members to find what works for them.*

Q: What's the purpose of the meetings?

A: *The ultimate purpose of the meetings is to provide support to each other as widows. As a group, you'll need to decide what other purposes you want to pursue.*

Q: What do we do when a group member doesn't follow the guidelines?

A: *While allowing for flexibility and individual differences, if a group member doesn't follow the guidelines agreed upon, you need to address the situation. Find out her reasons for non-compliance. If her lack of adherence to the guidelines interferes with the functioning of the group, you may need to ask her to leave.*

Q: How long should the group stay together?

A: *This is entirely up to the group. Most groups stay together as long as the individual members are receiving some benefit from their participation and commitment. If you trust your intuition, you'll know when it's time to dissolve the group.*

Q: How do we choose the topics and activities for each meeting?

A: *The host can select. The discussion leader can select. An individual member can select. The group can consensually select. Perhaps a list of suggested topics and activities is developed when the group forms. Then at the end of each meeting, the topic for the next meeting is selected. There's no one right way to do this. Just make*

Barbara Whitman Gaeta and Susan Whitman

sure the method you use is agreeable to all of the group members. Be creative!

Q: What do we do if one of our members remarries?

A: *Throw a party! Celebrate! As a group, you decide the qualifications for membership. Don't disqualify the member just on the basis of the marriage. Give her continued membership thoughtful consideration. Again, this is a group decision. It's also likely the former widow will choose to exit on her own.*

Q: As the host, do I always have to be in charge of facilitating the meeting?

A: *No. It's highly recommended that you share this responsibility by designating a different discussion leader for each meeting. As the host, you're responsible for taking care of the logistics.*

Q: If we need help, is there someone we can contact?

A: *Yes. You can contact us through the Wit & Wisdom website at* www.Wit&Wisdom.com *or you can call us at our toll-free number,...*

You'll notice that most of our answers are in the "it's up to you" category. And, how your group is formed and gels really is up to the group. It will take on a life of its own. The guidelines we're sharing will help you keep the group grounded and focused.

By sponsoring a Widows' Support Group, you will be providing a valuable service to widows, their families, and your community.

Chapter 10
Strategies for Creating Life Anew

Throughout this book, we've suggested a number of strategies for moving forward, for creating life anew. Here's a compilation of the most important ones we've suggested for your consideration.

Allow yourself to grieve in your own way, inquire, search, and find peace.

Honor your past, present, and future relationships.

Never give up on yourself and your abilities to create life anew.

Take risks and watch out for the unscrupulous at the same time.

Honor and release the past so you can move on to a new life.

Walk your own way.

Seek professional guidance with regard to financial, emotional, and spiritual issues.

Seek out a mentor to help you through the dark times.

Provide support for other widows.

Look for the wit and wisdom in every experience.

For Widows with Children

Many widows have to deal with their grief while responding to the needs of their young children. It's important to keep the memory of their father alive.

➔ **Consider...**

1. Share your husband's dreams with them. Tell them how he pursued them.

2. Create memory books with both pictures of their dad and themselves. Write captions with time, place, and situation to bolster their memories.

3. Help them create a memorial or altar in memory of their dad.

4. Allow them to keep possessions that hold meaning for them.

5. Answer their questions about the life and death of their father.

6. If you remarry, assure them that their father is still their father and that they have the fortune of having two men during their lives who love and care for them.

For Widows Who Remarry

Many widows will remarry. (Now that's cool!) When you realize your relationship could lead to a marriage, discuss how the both of you feel about death.

➔ **Consider…**

1. Agree that your last words at the end of the day be a tender "I love you."

2. Express your love through all of your actions.

3. Find out how he feels about life support. Both of you need to have a living will.

4. Talk about what to do when your partner dies.

5. Ask about funeral arrangements. Do you want a memorial service? Do you want to be cremated? Where do you want to be buried? Do you want to donate any of your body parts?

6. Talk about how you feel about another marriage.

7. Talk about the possessions, how to dispose of them.

8. Explore ways to deal with the grief of losing one another.

9. Express what you want for your partner if you die first.

It's our desire that the wit and wisdom we've offered have been meaningful for you. Perhaps you've laughed and cried with us as you've faced some of your issues through the stories we've told. The bottom line is this: Your life is yours, and you can live it anyway you want to. Walk your own way with wit into wisdom.

Barbara Whitman Gaeta and Susan Whitman

Epilogue

While watching the delicate blossoms of our African violets turn their faces to the morning light, I'm reminded that we must always reach out to life. When we do, life reaches out to us.

Sometimes I wonder what our lives would have been like if Dad had not died that morning in May. Yet, his death has helped me create a constant awareness of the richness of life.

Whenever I pass a flower, I stop to enjoy its color and fragrance. Whenever I meet a stranger, I look into her eyes finding the joy of recognizing a fellow seeker. I treasure every moment with the people I love. I make every effort to be available for whatever the present moment may offer. How do you feed your Spirit?

The world is abundant with constant reminders that everything living also dies and lives again in new form. When we feel as if our spirits are dying, we need to remember that the new form is waiting.

If we hide from life and the light, we wither away, just like a violet in the dark.

When you're standing on the edge of that cliff of grief and pain, faith in life and all that it can offer will be the wings to support you when you fall.

Better yet, jump off that cliff...into life and the unimaginable, turning your face to the morning light.

Barbara Whitman Gaeta and Susan Whitman

About The Authors

Widow Barbara Whitman Gaeta and widow-to-be Susan Whitman have formed a mother-daughter team to create a greater awareness about the emotional and spiritual needs of widows. Gaeta's husband of 40 years died suddenly in 1986, six months after her mother became a widow. Whitman's husband is 14 years her senior, making her impending widowhood very likely. Because of the widow experience, Gaeta's journey with Whitman changed them both in ways that only widows and their families can understand.

Gaeta, widowed for ten years and now happily re-married to a man twelve years her junior, had a facelift, colored her hair, got a small tattoo, and joined a naturist club . . . things she would have never thought about doing if she had not become a widow. These were ways she celebrated the fact that life continues when one mate dies. As an entertainer, she has a delightful sense of humor that engages her audiences. She epitomizes what *Wit & Wisdom for Widows*: *Beginning Anew* is all about – creating the life you want to live.

Gaeta has been engaged in research about widows since her husband died. Together with Whitman, they have created a workshop for widows to address their needs and concerns. They've interviewed numerous widows about their experiences, shared their own, and are perpetuating that spiritual bond of knowing and appreciation in the widow community.

Professionally Gaeta, now a consultant in volunteer program management, has worked with diverse organizations. She's served on boards for the American Red Cross, First United Methodist Church, and Epilepsy League. She's been the spokesperson for the United Way of Oakland (CA), American Red Cross, Epilepsy League, Oakland (CA) Unified Schools, and the Alzheimer's Association.

Gaeta has been honored as the Woman of Achievement for Business and Professional Women (Los Gatos, CA), awarded the Golden Rule Award by J.C. Penney for community service, and received the ten Gallon Blood Donor recognition by the American Red Cross. She worked on the National Red Cross Disaster Relief Team in Alaska in 1967. She has been writing journals, stories, and poems for many years.

Whitman, happily married for sixteen years, is also an engaging and entertaining speaker. She observed what could be construed as strange behavior for her mother, a woman in her mid-50s, with delight and support. Her relationship with her own husband has been significantly enhanced because of her mother's experience, appreciating every moment that she has with her husband and celebrating each day for the joy it brings. She encourages others to look at life in a similar way, recognizing that fate, old age, disease, or disaster could end her mate's life on this Earth at any moment. Her interest in widows' issues began when her mother became a widow and she realized she, too, would become a widow one day.

Whitman is an organizational development consultant and owner of Dynamic Teams. She's an active member and Certified Lay

Speaker for the United Methodist Church. She was an elected official as city councilwoman for Pacific Grove (CA) for eight years, serving on various committees. She has served in leadership roles for numerous community organizations. She has made hundreds of speeches to government, community, religious, and professional groups on topics of government issues, leadership, women in politics, and professional development.

Whitman has been honored as Woman of the Year by the Business and Professional Women's Association, Housing Advocate of 1990 by Monterey/Carmel Council of Real Estate Boards, and Woman of Achievement by Soroptimist of the Monterey Peninsula.

www.ingramcontent.com/pod-product-compliance
Lightning Source LLC
Chambersburg PA
CBHW030400290526
45785CB00004B/1834